Sales Basics for

Private

Investigators

Proven Sales Strategies for PI's

D1558886

John L. Morris

Table of Contents

INTRODUCTION

If Marketing is the heartbeat for a company, sales would be the lifeblood. Both marketing and sales go hand in hand, symbiotic yet not the same. You want to gear your marketing to get customers "in the door" or make your phone ring. After that, your sales hat must go on, and then the fun begins.

Learning proper sales techniques is crucial in any entrepreneurial business endeavor, and the business of private investigations is no different. This book will walk you through simple and proven steps to help ensure your sales game is up to snuff. Having a poorly designed sales plan can lead to disaster. Having a well-thought-out sales plan will give you an advantage over your competitors.

As with all plans for your business, your sales plan should be one that can be evaluated and changed as needed.

No matter how good your sales plan is, no matter how good of a salesperson you are, there will come a time when business situations will change. Your sales plan should allow for revisions with changing times. Modifications to your sales plan should be necessary for the business, and not on the whim to support your desires.

As with all of your business plans, your sales plan is YOUR sales plan. Taking steps to put together your sales plan is the first step in moving your company forward. Get ready for your big sales boom; your future is about to begin.

CHAPTER 1

WHAT AM I SELLING?

One of the biggest challenges every PI business faces is answering the question of "What am I selling?" No matter what services you provide, you probably have a good idea of what your company's hourly fees will be. The challenging "What" is more like "How Much."

There are first the one-off services, as I like to call them. These are services with a flat fee like process serving, background checks, and skip traces. One-Off serves usually have a flat fee tied to them, and they may have multiple levels of each service as well. For instance, the process serving flat fee might be $85.00, but an Expedited is $125.00, and a Same-Day Rush is $175.00.

For all of your one-off services, you should have an easily accessible rate chart for your reference. I never suggest providing this chart to clients. If they need pricing on particular services, you should give that to them directly. By giving them the price directly, you now have the opportunity to "Close the Sale." If you provide a rate chart, they can more easily comparison shop at any time, and your rate sheet cannot step in and close that sale for you. Remember, the key to increased revenues and sales is closing the deal.

Appendix A has a sample rate sheet for your review. You can use this sample to create your rate sheet for your reference. Once you have this, make sure you have a copy easily accessible at your desk and your fingertips if you are away from your desk. I usually recommend having a printed copy on the wall near to your desk so you can glance over when talking to the client on the phone. An electronic copy is good to have access to from your smartphone, tablet, or laptop. You can utilize any of the many cloud services out there to access certain electronic documents like your rate sheet.

But what about those other services that have hourly fees attached to them? How do you sell those to the client? This age-old question is best answered, NOT by the hour.

If you sell by the hour, you open the door for the client to just price shop, and price shop is what customers do best. Clients do not understand the complexity of an investigation, which leads them to determine the value at the lowest common denominator. Often, the only denominator most clients know regarding private investigators is the hourly fee. When they get on the search engines and search "how much does a private investigator cost," they will usually see hourly fee range results.

To overcome this, the best way for you to sell is by the job or by retainer. You will need to do some homework regarding selling to the client by the assignment or retainer. You need to know the typical time requirements for the type of investigative services you will be providing to your client. I always suggest having prices that will get all or most of the job done. Using prices that "get things started" can become problematic many times.

If you provide domestic surveillance services at $100.00 per hour, I suggest having three price points for the customer. Providing them options to choose from with different budgets can be very advantageous.

Three Day surveillance - $2,700.00 - Includes three 8 hour days plus mileage, travel time, report time, and video time.

Two Day surveillance - $1,800.00 - Includes two 8 hour days plus mileage, travel time, report time, and video time.

One Day surveillance - $900.00 - Includes one 8 hour day plus mileage, travel time, report time, and video time.

Make sure your prices cover everything you can think of and adjust as needed. In the example, we have an extra $100.00 for mileage, travel time, report, and video time. Is this enough revenue to cover the time for completing those duties? Evaluating the entire case and all of the assignment's complexities will help you decide the total cost for your client.

Set the tone upfront for case implementation with full case pricing. You can have many different options, such as 4 hour days, 6 hour days, or multiple investigators. Have as many options as you need, but try to have three choices for the client to choose from. More than three options can confuse clients, and less than three can appear to be too small of a pool. Full case pricing is a comfortable lead-in for the retainer discussion as well.

CHAPTER 2

FIRST CONTACT

A tremendous consideration in the sales cycle is the initial communication with the client. How will you be presenting your services to your clients? As a general rule of thumb, most private investigation businesses have the first contact over the phone. I always recommend targeting phone calls over other means of communication.

It is easy to put a chatbox on your website or a contact us form for the client to fill out and even an email address for them to send inquiries. Without direct contact, like over the phone or in person, the likelihood of closing the sale is severely low.

Imagine if you get an email from a company you are discussing business with, and the last line is, "Which option works best for you?" As the client, you are in full control of the conversation and the sale. You can choose to go with an option, offer counter options, go price shopping with competitors, or ignore it completely. As the lead salesperson in your business, your job is to close the deal, not send out proposals.

Emails do not close sales; chatboxes do not close deals; people make the deal happen. Gear your marketing to making your phone ring, and your job as the sales manager becomes a lot easier.

Once you have spoken with your client on the phone and closed the sale, it will become apparent if an in-person meeting will be necessary to finalize the deal. With today's world of ever-evolving e-solutions, it is easy to take care of business electronically.

CHAPTER 3

PHONE SALES TECHNIQUES

From the moment you answer your phone, you should always have your sales hat on. Answer your phone like a business. (with a smile and genuine sincerity) "Thank you for calling my private eye business. This is John. How can I help you?"

Once the client starts talking, let them. Listening is key to a good investigator on many levels and a necessity for an excellent salesperson. Always have a pen and paper handy for taking notes. As the client is talking, jot down notes, underline or asterisk vital things they say. Also, write your questions to the side, but wait to ask them. You want the customer to tell you as much upfront as possible. No interruptions allow for good information gathering and time for you to process the client's situation.

When is the customer done talking? Great question, and one that deserves an answer. I always wait until a second or two of silence passes before I start talking. Then the first words out of my mouth are usually something like, "Thanks for providing me all of that information. I know how hard it is for you to deal with this. We deal with situations like yours often."

Your concern needs to be genuine. It cannot just be a sales pitch intro. No matter what the situation is, no matter how many times you have worked similar cases, for your client, this is many times the very first time for them. Your first job is to make them comfortable speaking with you openly about their situation. Not only is it the first time they have had to deal with what is occurring in their life, but it is often also one the most challenging and traumatic times of their lives. Now, they have to share all of the gory details and problems of their experience with strangers. And to top it off, they worry about their financial stability through the process.

Next, you need to ask for more details. Asking these questions can be challenging, but it gets you the information you need to determine what course of action they need. You want to have as much information as possible to make an educated calculation of the cost for their investigation. Start to formulate potential investigative plans in writing. If it is a child custody situation, ask engaging and intuitive questions.

Where does the other parent live?

Who else lives with him or her?

Does he or she work?

What specific days of the week concern you?

How often does he or she get the kids?

Are grandparents or other relatives involved with the children regularly?

Keeping clients engaged is essential through this process. Reiterate what they have told you. Reiterating your customer's comments gets confirmation that you have the facts straight, and it gives the customer confidence that you are listening.

Okay, so he has the kids every other weekend. Does he have them this coming weekend or next?

You said she usually stops at the liquor store after work. What liquor stores does she typically frequent?

When the kids are with her, is her boyfriend usually at the house?

What time does he go to work and get off?

Now you have some more information, and you have gained some trust in the customer. It is now time to start formulating your plan for the investigation. But wait, do not throw out all of the options right away. It would help if you had a little more information. You can now start talking about what you think might be the solution.

"Mr. Customer, we deal with a lot of situations like this. As a general rule, we usually suggest surveillance to gather the necessary evidence. Is surveillance something you are considering?"

"Okay, we can do that. Do you currently have an attorney, and have you consulted with your attorney about conducting surveillance?"

Gathering information about the legal status of their case is vital. If the client has an attorney and has not consulted with their attorney about the situation, I often suggest that they speak with their attorney first. I make this suggestion to help ensure I am not wasting their hard-earned money. Sometimes their attorney may be taking the case in a different direction, and if they hire you for surveillance, the attorney may never seriously look at that evidence. On occasion, their attorney may have told them to talk to a PI about conducting surveillance, which is useful information.

Now before you discuss options, there is one more question that needs answering.

"Mr client, we have several options available to discuss. What budget do you have in mind for this?"

Now you have taken the lead fully in the discussion. You have built the pathway to get to the money talk. Usually, when I ask about the budget, I get answers like "I don't know, that is one of my questions." On occasion, though, a client will throw out a number. It is always good if they have a number in mind, as you can use this to provide them with options that fit their budget.

Whether they have or do not have a budget, it is always good to prepare three choices. If they have a dollar amount in mind, give them options with the upper range towards the top of their budget. Some may think it is better to have it in the middle. However, many times customers that have a good idea of what they are willing to spend will want to look at a "let's do this first' scenario.

If we look at our previous example, we have 1, 2, or 3 days of surveillance at $900, $1,800, and $2,700. If the customer says I was hoping to stay under $3,000, then this is perfect. Chances are they would either go with option three or start with option two. Rarely do they take the cheapest option.

If the client has a higher budget in mind, then you can adjust as needed. If they say, I was hoping to keep it under $5,000. You might propose these options.

Six Day surveillance - $5,400.00 - Includes six 8 hour days, mileage, travel time, report, and video.

Five Day surveillance - $4,500.00 - Includes five 8 hour days, mileage, travel time, report, and video.

Two Day surveillance - $1,800.00 - Includes twoe 8 hour days, mileage, travel time, report, and video.

In doing this, you have provided two options that fit close to their expectations and a third that is far less than what they probably desire. You might also bump up the lower ones in price.

Six Day surveillance - $5,400.00 - Includes six 8 hour days, mileage, travel time, report, and video.

Five Day surveillance - $4,800.00 - Includes five 8 hour days, mileage, travel time, report, and video.

Two Day surveillance - $2,000.00 - Includes two 8 hour days, mileage, travel time, report, and video.

Many times PI's have higher hourly rates for smaller jobs. In all actuality, the setup, case management, and wrap up time for the cases are very similar, so the percentage of time utilized is higher and can take away resources from fieldwork.

John L. Morris

Chapter 4

CLOSING THE SALE

Now you should have your options ready to present to your client. These calls take from 15 minutes to an hour on average to get to the point of closing. In my experience, the longer I keep the customer engaged, the higher percentage I have of closing the deal. That is if the conversation is of value. If you are talking to hear yourself talk, it could be detrimental to the task.

Now, the time has come. It is time to throw out the numbers. The presentation needs to be clear, concise, and to the point with something like this.

"Mrs. customer, this is what we can do for you. We can initiate covert surveillance at your ex-husbands' house on the weekends he has the kids, starting this weekend. I know finances are a concern for you, especially considering he hasn't been paying full

child support. With that in mind, I have prepared three options for you. Option one is a more aggressive investigation. This investigation would include three days of surveillance. I would suggest to spread these out over two weekends to ensure the integrity of the investigation. The cost for this is $2,700.00. I know this is a lot of money. This investigation includes three full eight hour days of surveillance, plus all travel time, mileage, case prep, report time, video, and photo prep time. Based on our experience, it is usually better to prove that the allegations occur on multiple occasions. This way, he cannot say, well, I was having a bad day. I never usually do that."

Now, the waiting game begins. You must pause. Silence and time are on your side. Wait for the client's response. I rarely provide all three of my options upfront. I know the silence on the phone is awkward, but after just a few seconds, your client will most likely respond in one of two ways. Optimistic and affirmative or reluctant due to cost.

If the client responds reluctantly due to cost, you can now continue the conversation with something like this.

"I understand that is a lot of money. What would work best for your budget?"

Now, if the customer throws out a number, you can formulate a plan based on that. If they reply with something like "I don't know, what are my other options?" you can respond like this.

"I know, $2,700.00 is a lot of money, and I fully understand your concerns. We also have two other options for you that that can help you get the evidence you need. We can do a two day or even a single day of surveillance in the same manner. We would still utilize the same expert surveillance investigator and provide all of the necessary reports, videos, and photos. Two-day surveillance would run $1,800.00, and a single day of surveillance is $900.00. Once completed, we could then discuss

the necessity for further investigation if desired. Which of these options would work best for you?"

Now it is time for some more of that awkward silence. Wait until the client gives you an answer. If the answer is something like "I need to give it some thought," then politely thank them and ask if you can follow up with them in a day or so. Most customers will choose one of the three options at this point if they have the funds and desire to move forward.

Other Sales Closing Techniques

Here are some other powerful techniques for closing the sale. When using these types of methods, keep in mind if you use them to force the sale, it will show through. You should also use ones that make sense for your particular business, services, and personality.

Time is Running Out - This is a little more difficult when selling services versus selling products. If you are selling products, it is easy to use this in the means of *"This is the last one at this low price"* But you can use other similar techniques such as *"We do have a 10% off Online Coupon that is running through today. If we move forward quickly, I can apply that to this investigation for you and save you some money"* I use this often for Process Serves and other One Off services as I usually run online coupons for those services. you could also say something like, *"If we move forward today with the contract, I can fast track your case to the front of the queue, and we can get started this weekend for you."*

Time is Running out techniques work as they create urgency in the matter, and if the client wants to get started right away or save some dollars, it may be of benefit. Beware though. This technique can seem pushy and forceful if misused.

The Case Summary close works best for me, usually. I reiterate the case to them like this *"We will schedule surveillance to start this weekend on your husband. We will be covering eight full hours Saturday and Sunday for a total of sixteen hours of covert surveillance at his residence. During the surveillance, we will follow him and the kids wherever they go and document everything we observe. We will also document any people he or the children are associated with and run basic backgrounds on those individuals. I can send the contract right away via Adobe E-Sign and email the retainer's invoice, which you can pay online. What email address would you like me to send those to?"*

Softer closes sometimes work much better as well. I often use something like, *"In your opinion, does the investigation I described make sense for your situation?"*

And if they seem to be balking at the price, you can use the Remove an Item technique. *"I know that is a lot of money, to be sure. I can offer you a discounted surveillance with just 4 hours each day. What four hour periods do you think would be best for each day?"* Cutting the case in half does take dollars, and potential profits, off the table, but it also helps you maintain your pricing integrity. If the investigation's total value is above what the customer can afford, then the risk is to lose it all. For me, I would prefer to work four hours at my regular full hourly rate, plus mileage and travel time, instead of working 8 hours at a discounted rate or worse, not get the case at all.

Another form of a softer close you might consider is *"If I could reduce the total price $900.00 would you want us to get started this weekend?"*

For One-Off services you provide, the phone sale can be relatively straightforward. Here is the technique I often use to great success. I will use Process Serving as an example. Client calls and inquires as to the cost of Process Serving. First, I ask a few qualifying questions, so I know how to price the serve.

"Absolutely, we can help you with that. What type of documents do you have to serve?"

"Great, about how many pages is it?"

"Perfect, where are they to be served?"

These questions let me know if I need to do any markups. For instance, restraining orders will usually be higher priced. It also allows me to see if it is under our 25-page max or if I need to charge a minimal large packet fee. And it lets me know what town it is going to or if it is outside of city limits in the country. We have different prices depending on these factors.

Next is my closing speel. *"Great, we can take care of that for you. Routine service is $85.00 that includes the first attempt* *in 3 days, and we do a total of 4 attempts for that $85.00. Routine service also includes the notarized affidavit of service. I can give you an email so you can email us the documents. Once we receive the documents, we will enter it into our system. Then you will receive an email with an invoice you can pay online. Once we have the documents and payment, we will schedule the work for you. If you grab a pen and paper real quick, I will give you the email address."*

Once they grab the paper and pen and write down your email address, they have effectively taken action, and you have closed the deal. Ninety percent of the time, I always get the documents emailed to me within 5 minutes. One of the biggest keys to closing the sale on the phone is getting the client to take some form of action. If you can convince the client to email or text you information about the case so you can prepare the investigation plan and contract, you will more likely than not get the sale.

The bottom line, one of the essential skills you need in sales as a private investigator, or in any line of work, is the ability to be skilled at closing the deal. Deal closing does not come easy for everyone, to be sure. Some people seem to be born with sales skills. But I know anyone, including you, can become the best salesperson around with some practice.

The best way for me is to write down a few of those closing techniques I want to try. Then I put that note on my monitor or desk. I have one for my One-Off Services like process serving, and another for regular investigations, and another for more extensive cases that come along. There is no one way to do it right all of the time.

Chapter 5

SOLIDIFY THE SALE

After you and the customer have decided which option works best, it is time to get to the nitty-gritty. Now you need to let the customer know the process going forward. This process should minimally include the client providing you with pertinent information, paying the retainer fee, and providing them with a contract. Once all of this is in place, you can then schedule the work. I never suggest to schedule work until you have the agreement, payment, and all needed information in hand. Moving forward with an investigation without any of these items can lead to complications down the road.

Customer Provided Information

I use a Customer Intake Form to gather pertinent information from my clients. Appendix B has a sample Customer Intake Form you can use or copy for your needs. The Intake Form is generic and can be adjusted on a per case basis as needed. In general, you will want the client to provide as much information as possible along with other pieces of information such as photos of individuals, pictures of vehicles, pertinent court documents, etc. The more information you can get, the better your case will be.

Contract

Once the client has provided you with all of the information, you can then prepare your contract for them. You may want to offer this first to ensure you have locked in the deal in some instances. Your agreement should be simple and to the point concerning the details. If you get too many details in the contract, it leaves a lot to be questioned. Your agreement should be explicit as to what the investigation will include.

Appendix B has a fundamental, minimalistic contract. I would not recommend using this sample contract for significant cases. You should always seek legal advice when deciding what type of contract or legal agreement you should use with your clients.

You can use either electronic means for your client to sign the contract, such as Adobe E-sign or other similar online products. You could also meet in person to have the client sign the contract. If at all possible, my preference is to meet in person with the client face to face. Meeting in person allows you to go over the contract in detail and ensure the client understands what the agreement says.

Another benefit of meeting the client in person is the collection of the retainer for the case. When I meet clients to take care of the contract and retainer, I request payment in cashiers check or money order made out to my business. If they wish to use a credit card, I can take those payments in person through my smartphone's credit card processing company. Alternatively, I can send them an invoice online ahead of time. I rarely suggest taking checks for payment for any services. If the client has "Buyers Remorse" for any reason, it is much easier to cancel a check, which can create many issues for you and your business.

When I have to use an electronic signature, I try to schedule some time on the phone with the client to go over the contract. A telephone conference with the client allows you to go over everything in the contract in detail and let your client ask questions.

CHAPTER 6

FOLLOW UPS

Another challenging task for most new entrepreneurs is to follow up with the clients that never made another contact. Following up can be very uncomfortable for many people. However, it can also become huge in adding to your bottom line when done correctly.

The reasons a client does not reach back to you may be numerous. They may have been too busy and forgot. They may have lost your contact information. It is always possible that they went with another company, but then it is always good to make a follow-up call and find out why they chose them over you even in those instances. Sometimes clients are trying to pull together the money for the case. I have even had cases where more stuff was happening that made them decide to do even more work, and they were trying to get all of the information together.

No matter the reason, if you never do follow-ups with prospective clients, you will never know what works, what needs to be improved, and why they decided not to work with your company. And even worse, you may never know they were ready to go. They just needed a little reminder. In my experience, I turn about 10% of all of my follow-ups into sales.

When you do the follow-up, you need to do it with discretion as well. If the client was going through some marital issues, then calling at dinner time might not be the most appropriate. Make sure you notate the date, day of the week, and time of the day when clients called you. I keep a running notebook for all of my customer inquiries with all of this information and more. Notes are great for future reference, and if you see the client called at 9:30 AM on Tuesday, then at 9:40 AM on Friday, it might be useful to try those follow-ups around the same time on the same days.

If your primary communication was through texts, you might want to follow up through text versus a phone call. Texting may be a more secure way of contact for the client and more convenient. Again, try to mimic the week's same days and times when the client reached out to you.

When I follow up, I say something like, "Hi, this is John with EVCO Investigations. We talked last week about doing some work for you. I just wanted to see what other questions you had for me." A leading question like this leaves the ball in their court. Notice, I don't ask, "Do you want to move forward?" I go with the assumption they may have questions. If the price is the problem, they may ask if I can do anything to bring the cost down. If they went with another investigative company, they will usually flat out say they decided to go with another firm. Hearing that the client chose your competitor is challenging, but it opens the opportunity for me to say, "Thanks, I appreciate you letting me know. If I may ask, why did you go with the other firm over us?" Almost all of the time, the customer will give you a genuine reason.

An essential key to follow-ups is to assume you may need to follow up later during the client's initial sales presentation. Early on, ask the client what the best way for you to communicate with them is. Asking the client allows them to let you know how and when you should contact them.

Make sure you also have a reason to reach out. Don't just call and say, *"I was just following up."* When you call your client back, you can say things like, *"In review of our weekend schedule, I noticed that we have a surveillance investigator available next weekend."*

You will also want to do some homework before the follow-up. Go through your notes from the conversation you had with them. Did you get the names of the children? You can always use that as an ice breaker, "How are things for you, Tommy and Stacey?" Demonstrating that you cared enough to remember is enormous in sales.

Setting the expectation for a follow up is always good practice too. In the event you do not close the sale on the first call, and this will often happen, ask the client if you can call in a day or two to see if they have more questions, then ask them if there is anything you can prepare for them for that meeting. Customers often need to think about things, mull it over, discuss it with spouses, siblings, parents, friends, attorneys, or other confidants in their life. Making these decisions in their life can be very confusing and challenging. If you can find ways to make it a tad more comfortable, that can go a long way in closing the sale.

CONCLUSION

The bottom line is the bottom line. Now you have the tools to assemble an effective sales plan that will positively affect your private investigation business's bottom line. Many a PI have come, and many a PI have gone because they could not effectively sell their services. You are now armed with the information you need for success in this never-ending battle of business sales.

No one ever said the PI business was easy, but then if it was, what fun would there be in that. Arming your sales department, your sales force, which is often just YOU, with proper tools and a well thought out plan and process for conducting sales, will ensure your success for years to come.

The most important advice I can give is that there is no one size fits all regarding being a successful salesperson. You will need to do some trial and error, some experimentation, and some techniques to see what works best. Start by taking the information provided in this book and carefully watching successful salespeople in the real world. What methods do they use? What words flow from their lips? Then formulate your ultimate sales strategy plan.

Practice makes perfect, as they say. Get in front of the mirror and run some of your planned techniques through some sales scenarios. What flows, what doesn't, what do you need to improve. The big thing is to keep pushing on, keep trying, but don't be THAT pushy sales guy. Clients will respect genuine honesty much more than a fast sales pitch. Now, answer that phone and make some sales.

APPENDIX A

SAMPLE RATE SHEET

STANDARD PROCESS SERVE	$85.00
EXPEDITED SERVE	$125.00
RUSH SERVE	$175.00
SURVEILLANCE SERVE (inc. 4 hours + mileage)	$500.00
BASIC SKIPTRACE (no hit $50.00)	$125.00
LOCATE INVESTIGATION (no hit $200.00)	$600.00

John L. Morris

APPENDIX B

CUSTOMER INTAKE FORM

Client's Name

Client's Address

Client's Phone #

Subject's Name

Subject's Address

Subject's Phone #

Subject's Relationship to the Client

Subject's Age and/or Date of Birth

Subject's Detailed Physical Description

Subject's Type of Vehicle, Color, and License Plate
If Known

Subject's Work Information - Hours of work if employed

Please state the purpose of the investigation in a short paragraph

Subject's Family & friends in the area - names & addresses if known

Subject's Other Information – Habits, smoking, drinking, etc. Favorite places to go, activities, driving pattern (fast, cautious, etc) etc.

APPENDIX C

SAMPLE INVESTIGATIVE SERVICES ENGAGEMENT AGREEMENT

This "Agreement" made this Wednesday, October 14, 2020 between Barnie Gordons, Hereafter known as "CLIENT", and EVCO LLC, hereafter known as "INVESTIGATIVE CONSULTANT".

Contact Information

CLIENT

Barnie Gordons

690 New Lake Dr.

Kansas City, KS 66000

INVESTIGATIVE CONSULTANT

EVCO LLC

PO Box 200926

Evans, CO 80620

(970) 658-3689

Services to be provided – The parties to this agreement agree that the INVESTIGATIVE CONSULTANT will provide the following services:

Conduct a Spot Check / Asset Location Investigation at 1100 Rambling Road Way., Evans, CO. 80620 where the CLIENT's Ex-Wife resides and is believed to be in possession of a Red Ford Pickup belonging to the client. This investigation will include up to 3 separate spot checks at differing times and days.

Service Payment – The CLIENT agrees to pay the INVESTIGATIVE CONSULTANT for its time, material, and services. Payment in full is due upon receipt of final invoice. A payment in the amount of $150.00 shall be required to initiate the agreement. The CLIENT agrees that the INVESTIGATIVE CONSULTANT will work to the best of his ability to perform the services within the scope of this agreement however the INVESTIGATIVE CONSULTANT makes no guarantees or warranties of service within the scope of this agreement.

CLIENT Signature _____

Printed Name _____ Date _____

EVCO LLC Signature _____

Printed Name _____ Date _____

*This is a sample of a simple user agreement NOT intended for legal purposes or usage.

Made in the USA
Columbia, SC
13 July 2022